Alchemy 100 Day Challenge Journal

BY
LETA HERMAN
&
JAYE MCELROY

Authors of
THROUGH THE MYSTERY GATE,
THE ENERGY OF LOVE,
and CONNECTING YOUR CIRCLE

For online videos, tutorials, and classes, visit:
AlchemyLearningCenter.com

Northampton, MA

The Alchemy 100 Day Challenge Journal
Copyright © 2023 by Leta Herman and Jaye McElroy

Born Perfect®
Northampton, MA 01060, USA
www.BornPerfectInk.com

Published in the United States of America
by Born Perfect®

ISBN: **978-0-9912366-7-1**

COMPANION GUIDE

*Many of you will be using this as a Companion Guide to the **Master Alchemy Program** or the **Inspired Action Podcast**.*

Whooo hooo... rock on!

*If you have any questions, please feel free to contact us at: **Info@AlchemyLearningCenter.com***

If you just found this journal, lucky you!
Your life is about to transform!

WHY 100 DAYS?

In this journal we borrow from the Daoist tradition of practicing specific activities, such as meditation and qi gong for 100 days.

The Chinese Philosophers believed multiples of the number 10, 100, or 10,000 are symbolic of an infinite number.

"YOUR INSPIRED CHALLENGE, IF YOU CHOOSE TO ACCEPT IT, IS TO SPEND THE NEXT 100 DAYS BEING FULLY ENGAGED, FULLY COMMITTED, AND FULLY PRESENT IN YOUR LIFE... USE THIS JOURNAL AS A TOOL TO RECORD YOUR JOURNEY." -- JAYE

If you choose to accept this challenge, you *will* transform on some level. You *will* be a different person, and that is the goal of Alchemy and transformation. It may be a big shift or a little shift, but when you commit to yourself... *shift happens.*

DON'T LET THE CHALLENGES OF THE PAST HOLD YOU BACK TODAY...

IT ALL STARTS WITH 100 DAYS...

HOW LONG WILL IT TAKE YOU TO GET THERE?

ALCHEMY 100 Challenge

A100C

This Alchemy100 Challenge is a spirit/mental challenge. These 100 days will challenge you to make the changes in your life that you want to make – change existing habits or patterns that don't positively serve you – and turn them into the life you truly want to live.

This challenge, if you choose to accept it, is a way to shake up your existence, push your comfort zone a little bit, and start you on the path that YOU choose to walk.

For this Alchemy100 Challenge, we will start as a group, and we can support each other until everyone has finished the challenge.

THIS IS A SELF-SUPPORTED GROUP CHALLENGE with love, kindness, affirmations, and accountability (in a good way!)

You can be a complete newbie to meditation or an experienced practitioner... both can complete this challenge. You can be someone who exercises all the time or someone who has not exercised in years... both can complete this challenge. You can be feeling healthy in your body or out of alignment in your body... both can complete this challenge.

A100C

Put all the excuses and reasons NOT to do this (it's too hard, it's too strict, I have no time, no energy, no money, too many projects, my partner, my kids, my job, I am out of shape, I can't meditate, etc...) aside for the next 100 days and TRANSFORM your life.

Don't let the struggles of the past hold you back today.

Let's put the FUN in the Fundamentals of this Challenge and do this together!

NOTE: Use common sense in designing your individual program for your health situation or consult a medical practitioner for specific advice.

A100C

FOR the next 100 days - You will:

Meditate: 30 mins EVERYDAY - you can split up the sessions to 15 mins in the AM and 15 mins in the PM One Alchemical meditation - based on what stage you are on. This is not a meditation program but a spirit/mental challenge.

Exercise: TWO - 30 min exercise sessions EVERYDAY. They can be: tai chi, qi gong, yoga, biking, running, hiking, walking, lifting weights... you can vary each day. One exercise session HAS to be outside. This is not an exercise program but a spirit/mental challenge.

Food: Pi Gu is an Alchemical approach to changing your diet by giving up a staple or food you don't feel is the best for you to eat. Sugar, grains, dairy, alcohol/drugs, etc. You can design your own eating program or follow an existing one, but it should be something that takes some effort and commitment to change. You can choose one of the popular diets: Keto, Paleo, Slow Carb, Fit for Life, Whole30, Weight Watchers, etc. Or create your own diet through eliminating specific items. You must commit to one food/diet program. This is not a diet program but a spirit/mental challenge.

A100C

Water: Drink ½ your body weight in ounces everyday (for example, if you weigh 140 lbs, you'd drink 70 ounces of water EVERYDAY). This is not a hydration program but a spirit/mental challenge.

Digital detox: No media for 1 hour when you wake up AND no media 1 hour before bed. This is not a detox program but a spirit/mental challenge.

Read: 10 pages a day in a real book (no audiobooks). This is not a reading program but a spirit/mental challenge.

Fast 1 day: (24 hours) a month - 5 Element Fast Recipe / or just water fast (use distilled water) - only mild exercise (such as walking) on this day. This is not a fasting program but a spirit/mental challenge.

Connection: Check in with the Alchemy100 group daily. You can get support, guidance, understanding, love, and kindness from others who are doing the program.

If you do not complete a FULL day, we invite you to join the RESET club and start your 100 Days over.

NOTE: Starting over isn't failing at all. Embrace the challenge of starting over in a gentle, kind, and loving way.

DAY

ALCHEMY **100** Challenge

GRATEFUL 4'S:

TODAY I WANT TO: ....

be	feel	think
....	....	....
....	....	....
....	....	....

ALCHEMY MEDITATION NOTES:

DIGITAL DETOX AM ☐
MEDITATION AM ☐
30 MINS MOVEMENT ☐
FOOD ☐
WATER ☐
OUTDOOR MOVEMENT ☐
DIGITAL DETOX PM ☐
READ 10 PAGES ☐
GROUP CONNECTION ☐
SLEEP ☐
FUN ☐
_____ ☐
_____ ☐
_____ ☐

DAY

ALCHEMY **100** Challenge

GRATEFUL 4'S:

TODAY I WANT TO: ....

be	feel	think
....	....	....
....	....	....
....	....	....

ALCHEMY MEDITATION NOTES:

DIGITAL DETOX AM ☐
MEDITATION AM ☐
30 MINS MOVEMENT ☐
FOOD ☐
WATER ☐
OUTDOOR MOVEMENT ☐
DIGITAL DETOX PM ☐
READ 10 PAGES ☐
GROUP CONNECTION ☐
SLEEP ☐
FUN ☐
_____ ☐
_____ ☐
_____ ☐

DAY

ALCHEMY **100** Challenge

GRATEFUL 4'S:

TODAY I WANT TO: ....

be	feel	think
....	....	....
....	....	....
....	....	....

ALCHEMY MEDITATION NOTES:

DIGITAL DETOX AM ☐
MEDITATION AM ☐
30 MINS MOVEMENT ☐
FOOD ☐
WATER ☐
OUTDOOR MOVEMENT ☐
DIGITAL DETOX PM ☐
READ 10 PAGES ☐
GROUP CONNECTION ☐
SLEEP ☐
FUN ☐
_____ ☐
_____ ☐
_____ ☐

DAY

ALCHEMY 100 Challenge

GRATEFUL 4'S:

TODAY I WANT TO: ....

be

feel

think

....

....

....

....

....

....

....

....

....

ALCHEMY MEDITATION NOTES:

DIGITAL DETOX AM ☐

MEDITATION AM ☐

30 MINS MOVEMENT ☐

FOOD ☐

WATER ☐

OUTDOOR MOVEMENT ☐

DIGITAL DETOX PM ☐

READ 10 PAGES ☐

GROUP CONNECTION ☐

SLEEP ☐

FUN ☐

_____ ☐

_____ ☐

_____ ☐

DAY

ALCHEMY**100**Challenge

GRATEFUL 4'S:

TODAY I WANT TO: ....

be	feel	think
....	....	....
....	....	....
....	....	....

ALCHEMY MEDITATION NOTES:

DIGITAL DETOX AM ☐

MEDITATION AM ☐

30 MINS MOVEMENT ☐

FOOD ☐

WATER ☐

OUTDOOR MOVEMENT ☐

DIGITAL DETOX PM ☐

READ 10 PAGES ☐

GROUP CONNECTION ☐

SLEEP ☐

FUN ☐

_____ ☐

_____ ☐

_____ ☐

ALCHEMY 100 Challenge

DAY

ALCHEMY **100** Challenge

GRATEFUL 4'S:

TODAY I WANT TO:

....

be	feel	think
....	....	....
....	....	....
....	....	....

ALCHEMY MEDITATION NOTES:

DIGITAL DETOX AM ☐
MEDITATION AM ☐
30 MINS MOVEMENT ☐
FOOD ☐
WATER ☐
OUTDOOR MOVEMENT ☐
DIGITAL DETOX PM ☐
READ 10 PAGES ☐
GROUP CONNECTION ☐
SLEEP ☐
FUN ☐
_____ ☐
_____ ☐
_____ ☐

DAY

ALCHEMY **100** Challenge

GRATEFUL 4'S:

TODAY I WANT TO: ....

be	feel	think
....	....	....
....	....	....
....	....	....

ALCHEMY MEDITATION NOTES:

DIGITAL DETOX AM ☐

MEDITATION AM ☐

30 MINS MOVEMENT ☐

FOOD ☐

WATER ☐

OUTDOOR MOVEMENT ☐

DIGITAL DETOX PM ☐

READ 10 PAGES ☐

GROUP CONNECTION ☐

SLEEP ☐

FUN ☐

_____ ☐

_____ ☐

_____ ☐

MEDITATION DOWNLOADS

NOTES / THOUGHTS / MUSINGS

WHAT INSPIRES YOU?

INSPIRED DOODLES

DRAWINGS /SKETCHES /DOODLES

WHAT INSPIRES YOU?

DAY

ALCHEMY **100** Challenge

GRATEFUL 4'S:

TODAY I WANT TO: ....

be	feel	think
....	....	....
....	....	....
....	....	....

ALCHEMY MEDITATION NOTES:

DIGITAL DETOX AM ☐
MEDITATION AM ☐
30 MINS MOVEMENT ☐
FOOD ☐
WATER ☐
OUTDOOR MOVEMENT ☐
DIGITAL DETOX PM ☐
READ 10 PAGES ☐
GROUP CONNECTION ☐
SLEEP ☐
FUN ☐
_____ ☐
_____ ☐
_____ ☐

DAY

GRATEFUL 4'S:

TODAY I WANT TO: ....

be   feel   think

....

....

....

ALCHEMY MEDITATION NOTES:

DIGITAL DETOX AM ☐
MEDITATION AM ☐
30 MINS MOVEMENT ☐
FOOD ☐
WATER ☐
OUTDOOR MOVEMENT ☐
DIGITAL DETOX PM ☐
READ 10 PAGES ☐
GROUP CONNECTION ☐
SLEEP ☐
FUN ☐
_____ ☐
_____ ☐
_____ ☐

ALCHEMY 100 Challenge

DAY

GRATEFUL 4'S:

TODAY I WANT TO: ....

be	feel	think
....	....	....
....	....	....
....	....	....

ALCHEMY MEDITATION NOTES:

DIGITAL DETOX AM ☐
MEDITATION AM ☐
30 MINS MOVEMENT ☐
FOOD ☐
WATER ☐
OUTDOOR MOVEMENT ☐
DIGITAL DETOX PM ☐
READ 10 PAGES ☐
GROUP CONNECTION ☐
SLEEP ☐
FUN ☐
_____ ☐
_____ ☐
_____ ☐

DAY

ALCHEMY **100** Challenge

GRATEFUL 4'S:

TODAY I WANT TO:

·····································

be   feel   think

·················   ·················   ·················

·················   ·················   ·················

·················   ·················   ·················

ALCHEMY MEDITATION NOTES:

DIGITAL DETOX AM ☐
MEDITATION AM ☐
30 MINS MOVEMENT ☐
FOOD ☐
WATER ☐
OUTDOOR MOVEMENT ☐
DIGITAL DETOX PM ☐
READ 10 PAGES ☐
GROUP CONNECTION ☐
SLEEP ☐
FUN ☐
_____ ☐
_____ ☐
_____ ☐

DAY

AL CHEMY **100** Challenge

GRATEFUL 4'S:

TODAY I WANT TO: ....

be	feel	think
....	....	....
....	....	....
....	....	....

ALCHEMY MEDITATION NOTES:

DIGITAL DETOX AM ☐

MEDITATION AM ☐

30 MINS MOVEMENT ☐

FOOD ☐

WATER ☐

OUTDOOR MOVEMENT ☐

DIGITAL DETOX PM ☐

READ 10 PAGES ☐

GROUP CONNECTION ☐

SLEEP ☐

FUN ☐

_____ ☐

_____ ☐

_____ ☐

ALCHEMY 100 Challenge

DAY

ALCHEMY **100** Challenge

GRATEFUL 4'S:

TODAY I WANT TO: ....

be	feel	think
....	....	....
....	....	....
....	....	....

ALCHEMY MEDITATION NOTES:

DIGITAL DETOX AM ☐

MEDITATION AM ☐

30 MINS MOVEMENT ☐

FOOD ☐

WATER ☐

OUTDOOR MOVEMENT ☐

DIGITAL DETOX PM ☐

READ 10 PAGES ☐

GROUP CONNECTION ☐

SLEEP ☐

FUN ☐

_____ ☐

_____ ☐

_____ ☐

ALCHEMY 100 Challenge

DAY

ALCHEMY 100 Challenge

GRATEFUL 4'S:

-
-
-
-

TODAY I WANT TO: ....

be

feel

think

ALCHEMY MEDITATION NOTES:

DIGITAL DETOX AM ☐
MEDITATION AM ☐
30 MINS MOVEMENT ☐
FOOD ☐
WATER ☐
OUTDOOR MOVEMENT ☐
DIGITAL DETOX PM ☐
READ 10 PAGES ☐
GROUP CONNECTION ☐
SLEEP ☐
FUN ☐
_____ ☐
_____ ☐
_____ ☐

MEDITATION DOWNLOADS

NOTES / THOUGHTS / MUSINGS

 WHAT INSPIRES YOU?

INSPIRED DOODLES

DRAWINGS /SKETCHES /DOODLES

WHAT INSPIRES YOU?

DAY

GRATEFUL 4'S:

TODAY I WANT TO: ....

be   feel   think

....

....

....

ALCHEMY MEDITATION NOTES:

DIGITAL DETOX AM ☐

MEDITATION AM ☐

30 MINS MOVEMENT ☐

FOOD ☐

WATER ☐

OUTDOOR MOVEMENT ☐

DIGITAL DETOX PM ☐

READ 10 PAGES ☐

GROUP CONNECTION ☐

SLEEP ☐

FUN ☐

_____ ☐

_____ ☐

_____ ☐

ALCHEMY 100 Challenge

DAY

ALCHEMY **100** Challenge

GRATEFUL 4'S:

TODAY I WANT TO:

....

be	feel	think
....	....	....
....	....	....
....	....	....

ALCHEMY MEDITATION NOTES:

DIGITAL DETOX AM ☐

MEDITATION AM ☐

30 MINS MOVEMENT ☐

FOOD ☐

WATER ☐

OUTDOOR MOVEMENT ☐

DIGITAL DETOX PM ☐

READ 10 PAGES ☐

GROUP CONNECTION ☐

SLEEP ☐

FUN ☐

_____ ☐

_____ ☐

_____ ☐

DAY

GRATEFUL 4'S:

TODAY I WANT TO: ....

be   feel   think

ALCHEMY MEDITATION NOTES:

DIGITAL DETOX AM ☐
MEDITATION AM ☐
30 MINS MOVEMENT ☐
FOOD ☐
WATER ☐
OUTDOOR MOVEMENT ☐
DIGITAL DETOX PM ☐
READ 10 PAGES ☐
GROUP CONNECTION ☐
SLEEP ☐
FUN ☐
_____ ☐
_____ ☐
_____ ☐

DAY

GRATEFUL 4'S:

TODAY I WANT TO:

....

be   feel   think

....

....

....

ALCHEMY MEDITATION NOTES:

DIGITAL DETOX AM ☐
MEDITATION AM ☐
30 MINS MOVEMENT ☐
FOOD ☐
WATER ☐
OUTDOOR MOVEMENT ☐
DIGITAL DETOX PM ☐
READ 10 PAGES ☐
GROUP CONNECTION ☐
SLEEP ☐
FUN ☐
_____ ☐
_____ ☐
_____ ☐

DAY

GRATEFUL 4'S:

TODAY I WANT TO: ....

be   feel   think

....

....

....

ALCHEMY MEDITATION NOTES:

DIGITAL DETOX AM ☐

MEDITATION AM ☐

30 MINS MOVEMENT ☐

FOOD ☐

WATER ☐

OUTDOOR MOVEMENT ☐

DIGITAL DETOX PM ☐

READ 10 PAGES ☐

GROUP CONNECTION ☐

SLEEP ☐

FUN ☐

_____ ☐

_____ ☐

_____ ☐

DAY

ALCHEMY **100** Challenge

GRATEFUL 4'S:

TODODAY I WANT TO:

....

be	feel	think
....	....	....
....	....	....
....	....	....

ALCHEMY MEDITATION NOTES:

DIGITAL DETOX AM ☐
MEDITATION AM ☐
30 MINS MOVEMENT ☐
FOOD ☐
WATER ☐
OUTDOOR MOVEMENT ☐
DIGITAL DETOX PM ☐
READ 10 PAGES ☐
GROUP CONNECTION ☐
SLEEP ☐
FUN ☐
_____ ☐
_____ ☐
_____ ☐

ALCHMY 100 Challenge

DAY

ALCHEMY 100 Challenge

GRATEFUL 4'S:

TODAY I WANT TO:

....

be   feel   think

....

....

....

ALCHEMY MEDITATION NOTES:

DIGITAL DETOX AM ☐
MEDITATION AM ☐
30 MINS MOVEMENT ☐
FOOD ☐
WATER ☐
OUTDOOR MOVEMENT ☐
DIGITAL DETOX PM ☐
READ 10 PAGES ☐
GROUP CONNECTION ☐
SLEEP ☐
FUN ☐
_____ ☐
_____ ☐
_____ ☐

MEDITATION DOWNLOADS

NOTES / THOUGHTS / MUSINGS

WHAT INSPIRES YOU?

INSPIRED DOODLES

DRAWINGS /SKETCHES /DOODLES

WHAT INSPIRES YOU?

DAY

ALCHEMY **100** Challenge

GRATEFUL 4'S:

TODAY I WANT TO:

....

be   feel   think

....

....

....

ALCHEMY MEDITATION NOTES:

DIGITAL DETOX AM ☐

MEDITATION AM ☐

30 MINS MOVEMENT ☐

FOOD ☐

WATER ☐

OUTDOOR MOVEMENT ☐

DIGITAL DETOX PM ☐

READ 10 PAGES ☐

GROUP CONNECTION ☐

SLEEP ☐

FUN ☐

_____ ☐

_____ ☐

☐

DAY

ALCHEMY **100** Challenge

GRATEFUL 4'S:

TODAY I WANT TO: ....

be   **feel**   **think**

....

....

....

ALCHEMY MEDITATION NOTES:

DIGITAL DETOX AM ☐
MEDITATION AM ☐
30 MINS MOVEMENT ☐
FOOD ☐
WATER ☐
OUTDOOR MOVEMENT ☐
DIGITAL DETOX PM ☐
READ 10 PAGES ☐
GROUP CONNECTION ☐
SLEEP ☐
FUN ☐
_____ ☐
_____ ☐
_____ ☐

DAY

ALCHEMY **100** Challenge

GRATEFUL 4'S:

TODAY I WANT TO: ....

be	feel	think
....	....	....
....	....	....
....	....	....

ALCHEMY MEDITATION NOTES:

DIGITAL DETOX AM ☐
MEDITATION AM ☐
30 MINS MOVEMENT ☐
FOOD ☐
WATER ☐
OUTDOOR MOVEMENT ☐
DIGITAL DETOX PM ☐
READ 10 PAGES ☐
GROUP CONNECTION ☐
SLEEP ☐
FUN ☐
_____ ☐
_____ ☐
_____ ☐

ALCHEMY 100 Challenge

DAY

GRATEFUL 4'S:

TODAY I WANT TO: ....

be	feel	think
....	....	....
....	....	....
....	....	....

ALCHEMY MEDITATION NOTES:

DIGITAL DETOX AM ☐
MEDITATION AM ☐
30 MINS MOVEMENT ☐
FOOD ☐
WATER ☐
OUTDOOR MOVEMENT ☐
DIGITAL DETOX PM ☐
READ 10 PAGES ☐
GROUP CONNECTION ☐
SLEEP ☐
FUN ☐
_____ ☐
_____ ☐
_____ ☐

MON TUES WEDS THUR FRI SAT SUN

DAY

ALCHEMY **100** Challenge

GRATEFUL 4'S:

TODAY I WANT TO: ....

be	feel	think
....	....	....
....	....	....
....	....	....

ALCHEMY MEDITATION NOTES:

DIGITAL DETOX AM ☐

MEDITATION AM ☐

30 MINS MOVEMENT ☐

FOOD ☐

WATER ☐

OUTDOOR MOVEMENT ☐

DIGITAL DETOX PM ☐

READ 10 PAGES ☐

GROUP CONNECTION ☐

SLEEP ☐

FUN ☐

_____ ☐

_____ ☐

_____ ☐

DAY

ALCHEMA **100** Challenge

MON TUES WEDS THUR FRI SAT SUN

GRATEFUL 4'S:

TODAY I WANT TO: ....

be	feel	think
....	....	....
....	....	....
....	....	....

ALCHEMY MEDITATION NOTES:

DIGITAL DETOX AM ☐
MEDITATION AM ☐
30 MINS MOVEMENT ☐
FOOD ☐
WATER ☐
OUTDOOR MOVEMENT ☐
DIGITAL DETOX PM ☐
READ 10 PAGES ☐
GROUP CONNECTION ☐
SLEEP ☐
FUN ☐
_____ ☐
_____ ☐
_____ ☐

ALCHEMY 100 Challenge

DAY

GRATEFUL 4'S:

TODAY I WANT TO: ....

be   feel   think

....

....

....

ALCHEMY MEDITATION NOTES:

DIGITAL DETOX AM ☐
MEDITATION AM ☐
30 MINS MOVEMENT ☐
FOOD ☐
WATER ☐
OUTDOOR MOVEMENT ☐
DIGITAL DETOX PM ☐
READ 10 PAGES ☐
GROUP CONNECTION ☐
SLEEP ☐
FUN ☐
_____ ☐
_____ ☐
☐

MEDITATION DOWNLOADS

NOTES / THOUGHTS / MUSINGS

 WHAT INSPIRES YOU?

INSPIRED DOODLES

DRAWINGS /SKETCHES /DOODLES

WHAT INSPIRES YOU?

DAY

ALCHEMY 100 Challenge

GRATEFUL 4'S:

TODY I WANT TO: ....

be	feel	think
....	....	....
....	....	....
....	....	....

ALCHEMY MEDITATION NOTES:

DIGITAL DETOX AM ☐
MEDITATION AM ☐
30 MINS MOVEMENT ☐
FOOD ☐
WATER ☐
OUTDOOR MOVEMENT ☐
DIGITAL DETOX PM ☐
READ 10 PAGES ☐
GROUP CONNECTION ☐
SLEEP ☐
FUN ☐
_____ ☐
_____ ☐
_____ ☐

DAY

ALCHEMY 100 Challenge

GRATEFUL 4'S:

TODAY I WANT TO:

....

be	feel	think
....	....	....
....	....	....
....	....	....

ALCHEMY MEDITATION NOTES:

DIGITAL DETOX AM ☐
MEDITATION AM ☐
30 MINS MOVEMENT ☐
FOOD ☐
WATER ☐
OUTDOOR MOVEMENT ☐
DIGITAL DETOX PM ☐
READ 10 PAGES ☐
GROUP CONNECTION ☐
SLEEP ☐
FUN ☐
_____ ☐
_____ ☐
_____ ☐

DAY

ALCHEMY 100 Challenge

GRATEFUL 4'S:

TODAY I WANT TO:

....

be	feel	think
....	....	....
....	....	....
....	....	....

ALCHEMY MEDITATION NOTES:

DIGITAL DETOX AM ☐
MEDITATION AM ☐
30 MINS MOVEMENT ☐
FOOD ☐
WATER ☐
OUTDOOR MOVEMENT ☐
DIGITAL DETOX PM ☐
READ 10 PAGES ☐
GROUP CONNECTION ☐
SLEEP ☐
FUN ☐
_____ ☐
_____ ☐
_____ ☐

DAY

ALCHEMY 100 Challenge

GRATEFUL 4'S:

TODAY I WANT TO: ....

be   feel   think

....

....

....

ALCHEMY MEDITATION NOTES:

DIGITAL DETOX AM ☐
MEDITATION AM ☐
30 MINS MOVEMENT ☐
FOOD ☐
WATER ☐
OUTDOOR MOVEMENT ☐
DIGITAL DETOX PM ☐
READ 10 PAGES ☐
GROUP CONNECTION ☐
SLEEP ☐
FUN ☐
_____ ☐
_____ ☐
_____ ☐

DAY

ALCHEMY 100 Challenge

GRATEFUL 4'S:

TODAY I WANT TO: ....

be	feel	think
....	....	....
....	....	....
....	....	....

ALCHEMY MEDITATION NOTES:

DIGITAL DETOX AM ☐
MEDITATION AM ☐
30 MINS MOVEMENT ☐
FOOD ☐
WATER ☐
OUTDOOR MOVEMENT ☐
DIGITAL DETOX PM ☐
READ 10 PAGES ☐
GROUP CONNECTION ☐
SLEEP ☐
FUN ☐
_____ ☐
_____ ☐
_____ ☐

ALCHEMY 100 Challenge

DAY

ALCHEMY **100** Challenge

GRATEFUL 4'S:

TODAY I WANT TO: ....

be	feel	think
....	....	....
....	....	....
....	....	....

ALCHEMY MEDITATION NOTES:

DIGITAL DETOX AM ☐
MEDITATION AM ☐
30 MINS MOVEMENT ☐
FOOD ☐
WATER ☐
OUTDOOR MOVEMENT ☐
DIGITAL DETOX PM ☐
READ 10 PAGES ☐
GROUP CONNECTION ☐
SLEEP ☐
FUN ☐
_____ ☐
_____ ☐
_____ ☐

DAY

GRATEFUL 4'S:

TODAY I WANT TO: ....

be   feel   think

....

....

....

ALCHEMY MEDITATION NOTES:

DIGITAL DETOX AM ☐
MEDITATION AM ☐
30 MINS MOVEMENT ☐
FOOD ☐
WATER ☐
OUTDOOR MOVEMENT ☐
DIGITAL DETOX PM ☐
READ 10 PAGES ☐
GROUP CONNECTION ☐
SLEEP ☐
FUN ☐
_____ ☐
_____ ☐
_____ ☐

ALCHEMY 100 Challenge

MEDITATION DOWNLOADS

NOTES / THOUGHTS / MUSINGS

 WHAT INSPIRES YOU?

INSPIRED DOODLES

DRAWINGS /SKETCHES /DOODLES

WHAT INSPIRES YOU?

DAY

ALCHEMY **100** Challenge

GRATEFUL 4'S:

TODAY I WANT TO: ....

be	feel	think
....	....	....
....	....	....
....	....	....

ALCHEMY MEDITATION NOTES:

DIGITAL DETOX AM ☐
MEDITATION AM ☐
30 MINS MOVEMENT ☐
FOOD ☐
WATER ☐
OUTDOOR MOVEMENT ☐
DIGITAL DETOX PM ☐
READ 10 PAGES ☐
GROUP CONNECTION ☐
SLEEP ☐
FUN ☐
_____ ☐
_____ ☐
_____ ☐

ALCHEMY 100 Challenge

DAY

ALCHEMY **100** Challenge

GRATEFUL 4'S:

TODAY I WANT TO:

....

be	feel	think
....	....	....
....	....	....
....	....	....

ALCHEMY MEDITATION NOTES:

DIGITAL DETOX AM ☐
MEDITATION AM ☐
30 MINS MOVEMENT ☐
FOOD ☐
WATER ☐
OUTDOOR MOVEMENT ☐
DIGITAL DETOX PM ☐
READ 10 PAGES ☐
GROUP CONNECTION ☐
SLEEP ☐
FUN ☐
_____ ☐
_____ ☐
_____ ☐

DAY

ALCHEMY **100** Challenge

GRATEFUL 4'S:

-
-
-
-

TODAY I WANT TO:

....

be   **feel**   **think**

....

....

....

ALCHEMY MEDITATION NOTES:

DIGITAL DETOX AM ☐
MEDITATION AM ☐
30 MINS MOVEMENT ☐
FOOD ☐
WATER ☐
OUTDOOR MOVEMENT ☐
DIGITAL DETOX PM ☐
READ 10 PAGES ☐
GROUP CONNECTION ☐
SLEEP ☐
FUN ☐
_____ ☐
_____ ☐
_____ ☐

DAY

ALCHEMY **100** Challenge

GRATEFUL 4'S:

TODAY I WANT TO: ....

be

feel

think

....

....

....

....

....

....

....

....

....

ALCHEMY MEDITATION NOTES:

DIGITAL DETOX AM ☐
MEDITATION AM ☐
30 MINS MOVEMENT ☐
FOOD ☐
WATER ☐
OUTDOOR MOVEMENT ☐
DIGITAL DETOX PM ☐
READ 10 PAGES ☐
GROUP CONNECTION ☐
SLEEP ☐
FUN ☐
_____ ☐
_____ ☐
_____ ☐

DAY

ALCHEMY 100 Challenge

GRATEFUL 4'S:

TODAY I WANT TO: _____

be   **feel**   **think**

....

....

....

ALCHEMY MEDITATION NOTES:

DIGITAL DETOX AM	☐
MEDITATION AM	☐
30 MINS MOVEMENT	☐
FOOD	☐
WATER	☐
OUTDOOR MOVEMENT	☐
DIGITAL DETOX PM	☐
READ 10 PAGES	☐
GROUP CONNECTION	☐
SLEEP	☐
FUN	☐
_____	☐
_____	☐
_____	☐

DAY

GRATEFUL 4'S:

TODAY I WANT TO: ....

be

feel

think

....

....

....

....

....

....

....

....

....

ALCHEMY MEDITATION NOTES:

DIGITAL DETOX AM ☐
MEDITATION AM ☐
30 MINS MOVEMENT ☐
FOOD ☐
WATER ☐
OUTDOOR MOVEMENT ☐
DIGITAL DETOX PM ☐
READ 10 PAGES ☐
GROUP CONNECTION ☐
SLEEP ☐
FUN ☐
_____ ☐
_____ ☐
_____ ☐

MON TUES WEDS THUR FRI SAT SUN

DAY

GRATEFUL 4'S:

- ☯
- ☯
- ☯
- ☯

TODAY I WANT TO: ....

be	feel	think
....	....	....
....	....	....
....	....	....

ALCHEMY MEDITATION NOTES:

DIGITAL DETOX AM ☐
MEDITATION AM ☐
30 MINS MOVEMENT ☐
FOOD ☐
WATER ☐
OUTDOOR MOVEMENT ☐
DIGITAL DETOX PM ☐
READ 10 PAGES ☐
GROUP CONNECTION ☐
SLEEP ☐
FUN ☐
_____ ☐
_____ ☐
_____ ☐

MEDITATION DOWNLOADS

NOTES / THOUGHTS / MUSINGS

WHAT INSPIRES YOU?

INSPIRED DOODLES

DRAWINGS /SKETCHES /DOODLES

WHAT INSPIRES YOU?

DAY

AL CHEMY **100** *Challenge*

GRATEFUL 4'S:

TODAY I WANT TO:

....

be	feel	think
....	....	....
....	....	....
....	....	....

ALCHEMY MEDITATION NOTES:

DIGITAL DETOX AM ☐
MEDITATION AM ☐
30 MINS MOVEMENT ☐
FOOD ☐
WATER ☐
OUTDOOR MOVEMENT ☐
DIGITAL DETOX PM ☐
READ 10 PAGES ☐
GROUP CONNECTION ☐
SLEEP ☐
FUN ☐
_____ ☐
_____ ☐
_____ ☐

DAY

ALCHEMY 100 Challenge

GRATEFUL 4'S:

TODAY I WANT TO:

be | feel | think

ALCHEMY MEDITATION NOTES:

DIGITAL DETOX AM ☐

MEDITATION AM ☐

30 MINS MOVEMENT ☐

FOOD ☐

WATER ☐

OUTDOOR MOVEMENT ☐

DIGITAL DETOX PM ☐

READ 10 PAGES ☐

GROUP CONNECTION ☐

SLEEP ☐

FUN ☐

_____ ☐

_____ ☐

_____ ☐

ALCHEMY 100 Challenge

DAY

ALCHEMY 100 Challenge

GRATEFUL 4'S:

TODAY I WANT TO: ....

be   feel   think

....

....

....

ALCHEMY MEDITATION NOTES:

DIGITAL DETOX AM ☐
MEDITATION AM ☐
30 MINS MOVEMENT ☐
FOOD ☐
WATER ☐
OUTDOOR MOVEMENT ☐
DIGITAL DETOX PM ☐
READ 10 PAGES ☐
GROUP CONNECTION ☐
SLEEP ☐
FUN ☐
_____ ☐
_____ ☐
_____ ☐

DAY

GRATEFUL 4'S:

TODAY I WANT TO: ....

be

feel

think

·········· ···

·········· ···

·········· ···

·········· ···

·········· ···

·········· ···

·········· ···

·········· ···

·········· ···

ALCHEMY MEDITATION NOTES:

DIGITAL DETOX AM ☐

MEDITATION AM ☐

30 MINS MOVEMENT ☐

FOOD ☐

WATER ☐

OUTDOOR MOVEMENT ☐

DIGITAL DETOX PM ☐

READ 10 PAGES ☐

GROUP CONNECTION ☐

SLEEP ☐

FUN ☐

_____ ☐

_____ ☐

_____ ☐

DAY

ALCHEMY **100** Challenge

GRATEFUL 4'S:

TODAY I WANT TO: ....

be   **feel**   **think**

....

....

....

ALCHEMY MEDITATION NOTES:

DIGITAL DETOX AM ☐

MEDITATION AM ☐

30 MINS MOVEMENT ☐

FOOD ☐

WATER ☐

OUTDOOR MOVEMENT ☐

DIGITAL DETOX PM ☐

READ 10 PAGES ☐

GROUP CONNECTION ☐

SLEEP ☐

FUN ☐

_____ ☐

_____ ☐

_____ ☐

DAY

ALCHEMY 100 Challenge

GRATEFUL 4'S:

TODAY I WANT TO: ....

be   feel   think

....

....

....

ALCHEMY MEDITATION NOTES:

DIGITAL DETOX AM ☐
MEDITATION AM ☐
30 MINS MOVEMENT ☐
FOOD ☐
WATER ☐
OUTDOOR MOVEMENT ☐
DIGITAL DETOX PM ☐
READ 10 PAGES ☐
GROUP CONNECTION ☐
SLEEP ☐
FUN ☐
_____ ☐
_____ ☐
_____ ☐

DAY

ALCHEMY **100** Challenge

GRATEFUL 4'S:

TODAY I WANT TO:

be	feel	think

ALCHEMY MEDITATION NOTES:

DIGITAL DETOX AM ☐

MEDITATION AM ☐

30 MINS MOVEMENT ☐

FOOD ☐

WATER ☐

OUTDOOR MOVEMENT ☐

DIGITAL DETOX PM ☐

READ 10 PAGES ☐

GROUP CONNECTION ☐

SLEEP ☐

FUN ☐

_____ ☐

_____ ☐

_____ ☐

ALCHEMY 100 Challenge

MEDITATION DOWNLOADS

NOTES / THOUGHTS / MUSINGS

 WHAT INSPIRES YOU?

INSPIRED DOODLES

DRAWINGS /SKETCHES /DOODLES

WHAT INSPIRES YOU?

DAY

ALCHEMY **100** Challenge

GRATEFUL 4'S:

TODAY I WANT TO:

....

be   feel   think

....

....

....

ALCHEMY MEDITATION NOTES:

DIGITAL DETOX AM ☐

MEDITATION AM ☐

30 MINS MOVEMENT ☐

FOOD ☐

WATER ☐

OUTDOOR MOVEMENT ☐

DIGITAL DETOX PM ☐

READ 10 PAGES ☐

GROUP CONNECTION ☐

SLEEP ☐

FUN ☐

_____ ☐

_____ ☐

_____ ☐

DAY

GRATEFUL 4'S:

TODAY I WANT TO: ....

be   feel   think

....

....

....

ALCHEMY MEDITATION NOTES:

DIGITAL DETOX AM ☐
MEDITATION AM ☐
30 MINS MOVEMENT ☐
FOOD ☐
WATER ☐
OUTDOOR MOVEMENT ☐
DIGITAL DETOX PM ☐
READ 10 PAGES ☐
GROUP CONNECTION ☐
SLEEP ☐
FUN ☐
_____ ☐
_____ ☐
_____ ☐

ALCHMY 100 Challenge

DAY

ALCHEMY **100** Challenge

GRATEFUL 4'S:

TODAY I WANT TO: ....

be   **feel**   **think**

....

....

....

ALCHEMY MEDITATION NOTES:

DIGITAL DETOX AM ☐
MEDITATION AM ☐
30 MINS MOVEMENT ☐
FOOD ☐
WATER ☐
OUTDOOR MOVEMENT ☐
DIGITAL DETOX PM ☐
READ 10 PAGES ☐
GROUP CONNECTION ☐
SLEEP ☐
FUN ☐
_____ ☐
_____ ☐
_____ ☐

DAY

ALCHEMY **100** Challenge

GRATEFUL 4'S:

TODAY I WANT TO: ....

be	feel	think
....	....	....
....	....	....
....	....	....

ALCHEMY MEDITATION NOTES:

DIGITAL DETOX AM ☐

MEDITATION AM ☐

30 MINS MOVEMENT ☐

FOOD ☐

WATER ☐

OUTDOOR MOVEMENT ☐

DIGITAL DETOX PM ☐

READ 10 PAGES ☐

GROUP CONNECTION ☐

SLEEP ☐

FUN ☐

_____ ☐

_____ ☐

_____ ☐

DAY

AL CHEMY **100** Challenge

GRATEFUL 4'S:

TODAY I WANT TO: ....

be   **feel**   **think**

ALCHEMY MEDITATION NOTES:

DIGITAL DETOX AM ☐
MEDITATION AM ☐
30 MINS MOVEMENT ☐
FOOD ☐
WATER ☐
OUTDOOR MOVEMENT ☐
DIGITAL DETOX PM ☐
READ 10 PAGES ☐
GROUP CONNECTION ☐
SLEEP ☐
FUN ☐
_____ ☐
_____ ☐
_____ ☐

DAY

GRATEFUL 4'S:

TODAY I WANT TO: ....

be feel think

....

....

....

ALCHEMY MEDITATION NOTES:

DIGITAL DETOX AM ☐
MEDITATION AM ☐
30 MINS MOVEMENT ☐
FOOD ☐
WATER ☐
OUTDOOR MOVEMENT ☐
DIGITAL DETOX PM ☐
READ 10 PAGES ☐
GROUP CONNECTION ☐
SLEEP ☐
FUN ☐
_____ ☐
_____ ☐
_____ ☐

DAY

ALCHEMY 100 Challenge

GRATEFUL 4'S:

TODAY I WANT TO:

be   feel   think

ALCHEMY MEDITATION NOTES:

DIGITAL DETOX AM ☐

MEDITATION AM ☐

30 MINS MOVEMENT ☐

FOOD ☐

WATER ☐

OUTDOOR MOVEMENT ☐

DIGITAL DETOX PM ☐

READ 10 PAGES ☐

GROUP CONNECTION ☐

SLEEP ☐

FUN ☐

_____ ☐

_____ ☐

_____ ☐

MEDITATION DOWNLOADS

NOTES / THOUGHTS / MUSINGS

 WHAT INSPIRES YOU?

INSPIRED DOODLES

DRAWINGS / SKETCHES / DOODLES

WHAT INSPIRES YOU?

DAY

ALCHEMY 100 Challenge

GRATEFUL 4'S:

TODAY I WANT TO: ....

be	feel	think
....	....	....
....	....	....
....	....	....

ALCHEMY MEDITATION NOTES:

DIGITAL DETOX AM ☐
MEDITATION AM ☐
30 MINS MOVEMENT ☐
FOOD ☐
WATER ☐
OUTDOOR MOVEMENT ☐
DIGITAL DETOX PM ☐
READ 10 PAGES ☐
GROUP CONNECTION ☐
SLEEP ☐
FUN ☐
_____ ☐
_____ ☐
_____ ☐

DAY

ALCHEMY **100** Challenge

GRATEFUL 4'S:

TODAY I WANT TO: ....

be

feel

think

....

....

....

....

....

....

....

....

....

ALCHEMY MEDITATION NOTES:

DIGITAL DETOX AM ☐

MEDITATION AM ☐

30 MINS MOVEMENT ☐

FOOD ☐

WATER ☐

OUTDOOR MOVEMENT ☐

DIGITAL DETOX PM ☐

READ 10 PAGES ☐

GROUP CONNECTION ☐

SLEEP ☐

FUN ☐

_____ ☐

_____ ☐

_____ ☐

ALCHEMY 100 Challenge

DAY

ALCHEMY **100** Challenge

GRATEFUL 4'S:

TODAY I WANT TO: ....

be	feel	think

....

....

....

ALCHEMY MEDITATION NOTES:

DIGITAL DETOX AM ☐

MEDITATION AM ☐

30 MINS MOVEMENT ☐

FOOD ☐

WATER ☐

OUTDOOR MOVEMENT ☐

DIGITAL DETOX PM ☐

READ 10 PAGES ☐

GROUP CONNECTION ☐

SLEEP ☐

FUN ☐

_____ ☐

_____ ☐

_____ ☐

DAY

ALCHEMY **100** Challenge

GRATEFUL 4'S:

TODAY I WANT TO: ....

be	feel	think
....	....	....
....	....	....
....	....	....

ALCHEMY MEDITATION NOTES:

DIGITAL DETOX AM ☐
MEDITATION AM ☐
30 MINS MOVEMENT ☐
FOOD ☐
WATER ☐
OUTDOOR MOVEMENT ☐
DIGITAL DETOX PM ☐
READ 10 PAGES ☐
GROUP CONNECTION ☐
SLEEP ☐
FUN ☐
_____ ☐
_____ ☐
_____ ☐

DAY

GRATEFUL 4'S:

TODAY I WANT TO: ....

be	feel	think

....

....

....

ALCHEMY MEDITATION NOTES:

DIGITAL DETOX AM ☐
MEDITATION AM ☐
30 MINS MOVEMENT ☐
FOOD ☐
WATER ☐
OUTDOOR MOVEMENT ☐
DIGITAL DETOX PM ☐
READ 10 PAGES ☐
GROUP CONNECTION ☐
SLEEP ☐
FUN ☐
_____ ☐
_____ ☐
_____ ☐

MON TUES WEDS THUR FRI SAT SUN

DAY

ALCHEMY **100** Challenge

GRATEFUL 4'S:

TODAY I WANT TO: ....

be   feel   think

....

....

....

ALCHEMY MEDITATION NOTES:

DIGITAL DETOX AM ☐
MEDITATION AM ☐
30 MINS MOVEMENT ☐
FOOD ☐
WATER ☐
OUTDOOR MOVEMENT ☐
DIGITAL DETOX PM ☐
READ 10 PAGES ☐
GROUP CONNECTION ☐
SLEEP ☐
FUN ☐
_____ ☐
_____ ☐
_____ ☐

DAY

ALCHEMY **100** Challenge

GRATEFUL 4'S:

TODAY I WANT TO:

....

be	feel	think

ALCHEMY MEDITATION NOTES:

DIGITAL DETOX AM ☐

MEDITATION AM ☐

30 MINS MOVEMENT ☐

FOOD ☐

WATER ☐

OUTDOOR MOVEMENT ☐

DIGITAL DETOX PM ☐

READ 10 PAGES ☐

GROUP CONNECTION ☐

SLEEP ☐

FUN ☐

_____ ☐

_____ ☐

_____ ☐

ALCHEMY 100 Challenge

MEDITATION DOWNLOADS

NOTES / THOUGHTS / MUSINGS

 WHAT INSPIRES YOU?

INSPIRED DOODLES

DRAWINGS /SKETCHES /DOODLES

WHAT INSPIRES YOU?

DAY

ALCHEMY **100** Challenge

GRATEFUL 4'S:

TODAY I WANT TO:

be

feel

think

ALCHEMY MEDITATION NOTES:

DIGITAL DETOX AM ☐
MEDITATION AM ☐
30 MINS MOVEMENT ☐
FOOD ☐
WATER ☐
OUTDOOR MOVEMENT ☐
DIGITAL DETOX PM ☐
READ 10 PAGES ☐
GROUP CONNECTION ☐
SLEEP ☐
FUN ☐
_____ ☐
_____ ☐
_____ ☐

DAY

ALCHEMY 100 Challenge

GRATEFUL 4'S:

TODAY I WANT TO:

be   **feel**   **think**

ALCHEMY MEDITATION NOTES:

DIGITAL DETOX AM ☐

MEDITATION AM ☐

30 MINS MOVEMENT ☐

FOOD ☐

WATER ☐

OUTDOOR MOVEMENT ☐

DIGITAL DETOX PM ☐

READ 10 PAGES ☐

GROUP CONNECTION ☐

SLEEP ☐

FUN ☐

_____ ☐

_____ ☐

_____ ☐

DAY

ALCHEMY **100** Challenge

GRATEFUL 4'S:

TODAY I WANT TO: ....

be	feel	think

ALCHEMY MEDITATION NOTES:

DIGITAL DETOX AM ☐
MEDITATION AM ☐
30 MINS MOVEMENT ☐
FOOD ☐
WATER ☐
OUTDOOR MOVEMENT ☐
DIGITAL DETOX PM ☐
READ 10 PAGES ☐
GROUP CONNECTION ☐
SLEEP ☐
FUN ☐
_____ ☐
_____ ☐
_____ ☐

MON TUES WEDS THUR FRI SAT SUN

DAY

ALCHEMY **100** Challenge

GRATEFUL 4'S:

TODAY I WANT TO:

be	feel	think

ALCHEMY MEDITATION NOTES:

DIGITAL DETOX AM ☐

MEDITATION AM ☐

30 MINS MOVEMENT ☐

FOOD ☐

WATER ☐

OUTDOOR MOVEMENT ☐

DIGITAL DETOX PM ☐

READ 10 PAGES ☐

GROUP CONNECTION ☐

SLEEP ☐

FUN ☐

_____ ☐

_____ ☐

_____ ☐

DAY

ALCHEMY 100 Challenge

GRATEFUL 4'S:

TODAY I WANT TO: ....

be   feel   think

....

....

....

ALCHEMY MEDITATION NOTES:

DIGITAL DETOX AM ☐
MEDITATION AM ☐
30 MINS MOVEMENT ☐
FOOD ☐
WATER ☐
OUTDOOR MOVEMENT ☐
DIGITAL DETOX PM ☐
READ 10 PAGES ☐
GROUP CONNECTION ☐
SLEEP ☐
FUN ☐
_____ ☐
_____ ☐
_____ ☐

DAY

ALCHEMY 100 Challenge

GRATEFUL 4'S:

TODAY I WANT TO: ....

be   feel   think

....

....

....

ALCHEMY MEDITATION NOTES:

DIGITAL DETOX AM ☐

MEDITATION AM ☐

30 MINS MOVEMENT ☐

FOOD ☐

WATER ☐

OUTDOOR MOVEMENT ☐

DIGITAL DETOX PM ☐

READ 10 PAGES ☐

GROUP CONNECTION ☐

SLEEP ☐

FUN ☐

_____ ☐

_____ ☐

_____ ☐

ALCHEMY 100 Challenge

DAY

ALCHEMY 100 Challenge

GRATEFUL 4'S:

TODAY I WANT TO: ....

be   feel   think

....

....

....

ALCHEMY MEDITATION NOTES:

DIGITAL DETOX AM ☐
MEDITATION AM ☐
30 MINS MOVEMENT ☐
FOOD ☐
WATER ☐
OUTDOOR MOVEMENT ☐
DIGITAL DETOX PM ☐
READ 10 PAGES ☐
GROUP CONNECTION ☐
SLEEP ☐
FUN ☐
_____ ☐
_____ ☐
_____ ☐

MEDITATION DOWNLOADS

NOTES / THOUGHTS / MUSINGS

 WHAT INSPIRES YOU?

INSPIRED DOODLES

DRAWINGS /SKETCHES /DOODLES

WHAT INSPIRES YOU?

DAY

ALCHEMY **100** Challenge

GRATEFUL 4'S:

TODAY I WANT TO: ....

be   **feel**   **think**

....

....

....

ALCHEMY MEDITATION NOTES:

DIGITAL DETOX AM ☐
MEDITATION AM ☐
30 MINS MOVEMENT ☐
FOOD ☐
WATER ☐
OUTDOOR MOVEMENT ☐
DIGITAL DETOX PM ☐
READ 10 PAGES ☐
GROUP CONNECTION ☐
SLEEP ☐
FUN ☐
_____ ☐
_____ ☐
_____ ☐

DAY

ALCHEMY **100** Challenge

GRATEFUL 4'S:

TODAY I WANT TO: ....

be   feel   think

ALCHEMY MEDITATION NOTES:

DIGITAL DETOX AM ☐
MEDITATION AM ☐
30 MINS MOVEMENT ☐
FOOD ☐
WATER ☐
OUTDOOR MOVEMENT ☐
DIGITAL DETOX PM ☐
READ 10 PAGES ☐
GROUP CONNECTION ☐
SLEEP ☐
FUN ☐
_____ ☐
_____ ☐
_____ ☐

DAY

ALCHEMY **100** Challenge

GRATEFUL 4'S:

TODAY I WANT TO: ....

be	feel	think
....	....	....
....	....	....
....	....	....

ALCHEMY MEDITATION NOTES:

DIGITAL DETOX AM ☐
MEDITATION AM ☐
30 MINS MOVEMENT ☐
FOOD ☐
WATER ☐
OUTDOOR MOVEMENT ☐
DIGITAL DETOX PM ☐
READ 10 PAGES ☐
GROUP CONNECTION ☐
SLEEP ☐
FUN ☐
_____ ☐
_____ ☐
_____ ☐

DAY

ALCHEMY 100 Challenge

GRATEFUL 4'S:

TODAY I WANT TO: ....

be	feel	think
....	....	....
....	....	....
....	....	....

ALCHEMY MEDITATION NOTES:

DIGITAL DETOX AM ☐
MEDITATION AM ☐
30 MINS MOVEMENT ☐
FOOD ☐
WATER ☐
OUTDOOR MOVEMENT ☐
DIGITAL DETOX PM ☐
READ 10 PAGES ☐
GROUP CONNECTION ☐
SLEEP ☐
FUN ☐
_____ ☐
_____ ☐
_____ ☐

DAY

ALCHEMY 100 Challenge

GRATEFUL 4'S:

TODAY I WANT TO: ....

be

feel

think

....

....

....

....

....

....

....

....

....

ALCHEMY MEDITATION NOTES:

DIGITAL DETOX AM	☐
MEDITATION AM	☐
30 MINS MOVEMENT	☐
FOOD	☐
WATER	☐
OUTDOOR MOVEMENT	☐
DIGITAL DETOX PM	☐
READ 10 PAGES	☐
GROUP CONNECTION	☐
SLEEP	☐
FUN	☐
_____	☐
_____	☐
_____	☐

DAY

ALCHEMY 100 Challenge

GRATEFUL 4'S:

TODAY I WANT TO: ....

be   **feel**   **think**

....

....

....

ALCHEMY MEDITATION NOTES:

DIGITAL DETOX AM ☐

MEDITATION AM ☐

30 MINS MOVEMENT ☐

FOOD ☐

WATER ☐

OUTDOOR MOVEMENT ☐

DIGITAL DETOX PM ☐

READ 10 PAGES ☐

GROUP CONNECTION ☐

SLEEP ☐

FUN ☐

_____ ☐

_____ ☐

_____ ☐

DAY

ALCHEMY **100** Challenge

GRATEFUL 4'S:

TODAY I WANT TO: ....

be   **feel**   **think**

....

....

....

ALCHEMY MEDITATION NOTES:

DIGITAL DETOX AM ☐
MEDITATION AM ☐
30 MINS MOVEMENT ☐
FOOD ☐
WATER ☐
OUTDOOR MOVEMENT ☐
DIGITAL DETOX PM ☐
READ 10 PAGES ☐
GROUP CONNECTION ☐
SLEEP ☐
FUN ☐
_____ ☐
_____ ☐
_____ ☐

MEDITATION DOWNLOADS

NOTES / THOUGHTS / MUSINGS

 WHAT INSPIRES YOU?

INSPIRED DOODLES

DRAWINGS /SKETCHES /DOODLES

WHAT INSPIRES YOU?

DAY

ALCHEMY 100 Challenge

GRATEFUL 4'S:

TODAY I WANT TO: ....

be	feel	think
....	....	....
....	....	....
....	....	....

ALCHEMY MEDITATION NOTES:

DIGITAL DETOX AM ☐
MEDITATION AM ☐
30 MINS MOVEMENT ☐
FOOD ☐
WATER ☐
OUTDOOR MOVEMENT ☐
DIGITAL DETOX PM ☐
READ 10 PAGES ☐
GROUP CONNECTION ☐
SLEEP ☐
FUN ☐
_____ ☐
_____ ☐
_____ ☐

DAY

ALCHEMY 100 Challenge

GRATEFUL 4'S:

TODAY I WANT TO: ....

be	feel	think
....	....	....
....	....	....
....	....	....

ALCHEMY MEDITATION NOTES:

DIGITAL DETOX AM ☐
MEDITATION AM ☐
30 MINS MOVEMENT ☐
FOOD ☐
WATER ☐
OUTDOOR MOVEMENT ☐
DIGITAL DETOX PM ☐
READ 10 PAGES ☐
GROUP CONNECTION ☐
SLEEP ☐
FUN ☐
_____ ☐
_____ ☐
_____ ☐

DAY

ALCHEMY 100 Challenge

GRATEFUL 4'S:

TODAY I WANT TO: ....

be	feel	think
....	....	....
....	....	....
....	....	....

ALCHEMY MEDITATION NOTES:

DIGITAL DETOX AM ☐

MEDITATION AM ☐

30 MINS MOVEMENT ☐

FOOD ☐

WATER ☐

OUTDOOR MOVEMENT ☐

DIGITAL DETOX PM ☐

READ 10 PAGES ☐

GROUP CONNECTION ☐

SLEEP ☐

FUN ☐

_____ ☐

_____ ☐

_____ ☐

DAY

ALCHEMY 100 Challenge

GRATEFUL 4'S:

TODAY I WANT TO:

....

be	feel	think
....	....	....
....	....	....
....	....	....

ALCHEMY MEDITATION NOTES:

DIGITAL DETOX AM ☐

MEDITATION AM ☐

30 MINS MOVEMENT ☐

FOOD ☐

WATER ☐

OUTDOOR MOVEMENT ☐

DIGITAL DETOX PM ☐

READ 10 PAGES ☐

GROUP CONNECTION ☐

SLEEP ☐

FUN ☐

_____ ☐

_____ ☐

_____ ☐

DAY

ALCHEMY 100 Challenge

GRATEFUL 4'S:

TODAY I WANT TO: _____

be	feel	think
....	....	....
....	....	....
....	....	....

ALCHEMY MEDITATION NOTES:

DIGITAL DETOX AM ☐

MEDITATION AM ☐

30 MINS MOVEMENT ☐

FOOD ☐

WATER ☐

OUTDOOR MOVEMENT ☐

DIGITAL DETOX PM ☐

READ 10 PAGES ☐

GROUP CONNECTION ☐

SLEEP ☐

FUN ☐

_____ ☐

_____ ☐

_____ ☐

DAY

ALCHEMY 100 Challenge

GRATEFUL 4'S:

TODAY I WANT TO: ....

be   feel   think

....

....

....

ALCHEMY MEDITATION NOTES:

DIGITAL DETOX AM ☐

MEDITATION AM ☐

30 MINS MOVEMENT ☐

FOOD ☐

WATER ☐

OUTDOOR MOVEMENT ☐

DIGITAL DETOX PM ☐

READ 10 PAGES ☐

GROUP CONNECTION ☐

SLEEP ☐

FUN ☐

_____ ☐

_____ ☐

_____ ☐

ALCHEMY 100 Challenge

DAY

ALCHEMY **100** Challenge

GRATEFUL 4'S:

TODAY I WANT TO:

be   **feel**   **think**

....

....

....

ALCHEMY MEDITATION NOTES:

DIGITAL DETOX AM ☐

MEDITATION AM ☐

30 MINS MOVEMENT ☐

FOOD ☐

WATER ☐

OUTDOOR MOVEMENT ☐

DIGITAL DETOX PM ☐

READ 10 PAGES ☐

GROUP CONNECTION ☐

SLEEP ☐

FUN ☐

_____ ☐

_____ ☐

_____ ☐

MEDITATION DOWNLOADS

NOTES / THOUGHTS / MUSINGS

WHAT INSPIRES YOU?

INSPIRED DOODLES

DRAWINGS /SKETCHES /DOODLES

WHAT INSPIRES YOU?

DAY

ALCHEMY **100** Challenge

GRATEFUL 4'S:

TODAY I WANT TO:

....

be   feel   think

....

....

....

ALCHEMY MEDITATION NOTES:

DIGITAL DETOX AM ☐
MEDITATION AM ☐
30 MINS MOVEMENT ☐
FOOD ☐
WATER ☐
OUTDOOR MOVEMENT ☐
DIGITAL DETOX PM ☐
READ 10 PAGES ☐
GROUP CONNECTION ☐
SLEEP ☐
FUN ☐
_____ ☐
_____ ☐
_____ ☐

DAY

ALCHEMY 100 Challenge

GRATEFUL 4'S:

TODAY I WANT TO:

....

be	feel	think
....	....	....
....	....	....
....	....	....

ALCHEMY MEDITATION NOTES:

DIGITAL DETOX AM ☐
MEDITATION AM ☐
30 MINS MOVEMENT ☐
FOOD ☐
WATER ☐
OUTDOOR MOVEMENT ☐
DIGITAL DETOX PM ☐
READ 10 PAGES ☐
GROUP CONNECTION ☐
SLEEP ☐
FUN ☐
_____ ☐
_____ ☐
_____ ☐

DAY

ALCHEMY **100** *Challenge*

GRATEFUL 4'S:

TODAY I WANT TO: ....

be	feel	think
....	....	....
....	....	....
....	....	....

ALCHEMY MEDITATION NOTES:

DIGITAL DETOX AM ☐

MEDITATION AM ☐

30 MINS MOVEMENT ☐

FOOD ☐

WATER ☐

OUTDOOR MOVEMENT ☐

DIGITAL DETOX PM ☐

READ 10 PAGES ☐

GROUP CONNECTION ☐

SLEEP ☐

FUN ☐

_____ ☐

_____ ☐

_____ ☐

DAY

ALCHEMY **100** Challenge

GRATEFUL 4'S:

TODAY I WANT TO: ....

be	feel	think
..................∞	..................∞	..................∞
..................∞	..................∞	..................∞
..................∞	..................∞	..................∞

ALCHEMY MEDITATION NOTES:

DIGITAL DETOX AM ☐
MEDITATION AM ☐
30 MINS MOVEMENT ☐
FOOD ☐
WATER ☐
OUTDOOR MOVEMENT ☐
DIGITAL DETOX PM ☐
READ 10 PAGES ☐
GROUP CONNECTION ☐
SLEEP ☐
FUN ☐
_____ ☐
_____ ☐
_____ ☐

DAY

ALCHEMY 100 Challenge

GRATEFUL 4'S:

TODAY I WANT TO:

....

be   feel   think

....

....

....

ALCHEMY MEDITATION NOTES:

DIGITAL DETOX AM ☐
MEDITATION AM ☐
30 MINS MOVEMENT ☐
FOOD ☐
WATER ☐
OUTDOOR MOVEMENT ☐
DIGITAL DETOX PM ☐
READ 10 PAGES ☐
GROUP CONNECTION ☐
SLEEP ☐
FUN ☐
_____ ☐
_____ ☐
_____ ☐

DAY

ALCHEMY **100** Challenge

GRATEFUL 4'S:

TODAY I WANT TO: ....

be	feel	think
....	....	....
....	....	....
....	....	....

ALCHEMY MEDITATION NOTES:

DIGITAL DETOX AM ☐

MEDITATION AM ☐

30 MINS MOVEMENT ☐

FOOD ☐

WATER ☐

OUTDOOR MOVEMENT ☐

DIGITAL DETOX PM ☐

READ 10 PAGES ☐

GROUP CONNECTION ☐

SLEEP ☐

FUN ☐

_____ ☐

_____ ☐

_____ ☐

DAY

ALCHEMY **100** Challenge

GRATEFUL 4'S:

TODAY I WANT TO:

....

be   feel   think

....

....

....

ALCHEMY MEDITATION NOTES:

DIGITAL DETOX AM ☐
MEDITATION AM ☐
30 MINS MOVEMENT ☐
FOOD ☐
WATER ☐
OUTDOOR MOVEMENT ☐
DIGITAL DETOX PM ☐
READ 10 PAGES ☐
GROUP CONNECTION ☐
SLEEP ☐
FUN ☐
_____ ☐
_____ ☐
_____ ☐

MEDITATION DOWNLOADS

NOTES / THOUGHTS / MUSINGS

 WHAT INSPIRES YOU?

INSPIRED DOODLES

DRAWINGS /SKETCHES /DOODLES

WHAT INSPIRES YOU?

DAY

ALCHEMY **100** Challenge

GRATEFUL 4'S:

-
-
-
-

TODAY I WANT TO: ....

be	feel	think
....	....	....
....	....	....
....	....	....

ALCHEMY MEDITATION NOTES:

DIGITAL DETOX AM ☐
MEDITATION AM ☐
30 MINS MOVEMENT ☐
FOOD ☐
WATER ☐
OUTDOOR MOVEMENT ☐
DIGITAL DETOX PM ☐
READ 10 PAGES ☐
GROUP CONNECTION ☐
SLEEP ☐
FUN ☐
_____ ☐
_____ ☐
_____ ☐

DAY

ALCHEMY **100** Challenge

GRATEFUL 4'S:

TODAY I WANT TO: ....

be	feel	think
....	....	....
....	....	....
....	....	....

ALCHEMY MEDITATION NOTES:

DIGITAL DETOX AM ☐

MEDITATION AM ☐

30 MINS MOVEMENT ☐

FOOD ☐

WATER ☐

OUTDOOR MOVEMENT ☐

DIGITAL DETOX PM ☐

READ 10 PAGES ☐

GROUP CONNECTION ☐

SLEEP ☐

FUN ☐

_____ ☐

_____ ☐

☐

ALCHEMY 100 Challenge

DAY

ALCHEMY **100** Challenge

GRATEFUL 4'S:

TODAY I WANT TO: ....

be	feel	think
....	....	....
....	....	....
....	....	....

ALCHEMY MEDITATION NOTES:

DIGITAL DETOX AM ☐
MEDITATION AM ☐
30 MINS MOVEMENT ☐
FOOD ☐
WATER ☐
OUTDOOR MOVEMENT ☐
DIGITAL DETOX PM ☐
READ 10 PAGES ☐
GROUP CONNECTION ☐
SLEEP ☐
FUN ☐
_____ ☐
_____ ☐
_____ ☐

DAY

4LCHEMY **100** Challenge

GRATEFUL 4'S:

TODAY I WANT TO:

....

be   feel   think

....

....

....

ALCHEMY MEDITATION NOTES:

DIGITAL DETOX AM ☐
MEDITATION AM ☐
30 MINS MOVEMENT ☐
FOOD ☐
WATER ☐
OUTDOOR MOVEMENT ☐
DIGITAL DETOX PM ☐
READ 10 PAGES ☐
GROUP CONNECTION ☐
SLEEP ☐
FUN ☐
_____ ☐
_____ ☐
_____ ☐

DAY

AL CHEMY 100 Challenge

GRATEFUL 4'S:

TODAY I WANT TO: ....

be   feel   think

....

....

....

ALCHEMY MEDITATION NOTES:

DIGITAL DETOX AM ☐

MEDITATION AM ☐

30 MINS MOVEMENT ☐

FOOD ☐

WATER ☐

OUTDOOR MOVEMENT ☐

DIGITAL DETOX PM ☐

READ 10 PAGES ☐

GROUP CONNECTION ☐

SLEEP ☐

FUN ☐

_____ ☐

_____ ☐

_____ ☐

DAY

ALCHEMY 100 Challenge

GRATEFUL 4'S:

TODAY I WANT TO: ....

be   feel   think

....

....

....

ALCHEMY MEDITATION NOTES:

DIGITAL DETOX AM ☐

MEDITATION AM ☐

30 MINS MOVEMENT ☐

FOOD ☐

WATER ☐

OUTDOOR MOVEMENT ☐

DIGITAL DETOX PM ☐

READ 10 PAGES ☐

GROUP CONNECTION ☐

SLEEP ☐

FUN ☐

_____ ☐

_____ ☐

_____ ☐

DAY

ALCHEMY 100 Challenge

GRATEFUL 4'S:

TODAY I WANT TO: _____

be	feel	think
....	....	....
....	....	....
....	....	....

ALCHEMY MEDITATION NOTES:

DIGITAL DETOX AM ☐

MEDITATION AM ☐

30 MINS MOVEMENT ☐

FOOD ☐

WATER ☐

OUTDOOR MOVEMENT ☐

DIGITAL DETOX PM ☐

READ 10 PAGES ☐

GROUP CONNECTION ☐

SLEEP ☐

FUN ☐

_____ ☐

_____ ☐

_____ ☐

DAY

ALCHEMY **100** Challenge

GRATEFUL 4'S:

TODAY I WANT TO: ....

be   feel   think

....

....

....

ALCHEMY MEDITATION NOTES:

DIGITAL DETOX AM ☐
MEDITATION AM ☐
30 MINS MOVEMENT ☐
FOOD ☐
WATER ☐
OUTDOOR MOVEMENT ☐
DIGITAL DETOX PM ☐
READ 10 PAGES ☐
GROUP CONNECTION ☐
SLEEP ☐
FUN ☐
_____ ☐
_____ ☐
_____ ☐

DAY

ALCHEMY **100** Challenge

GRATEFUL 4'S:

TODAY I WANT TO: ....

be	feel	think
....	....	....
....	....	....
....	....	....

ALCHEMY MEDITATION NOTES:

DIGITAL DETOX AM ☐
MEDITATION AM ☐
30 MINS MOVEMENT ☐
FOOD ☐
WATER ☐
OUTDOOR MOVEMENT ☐
DIGITAL DETOX PM ☐
READ 10 PAGES ☐
GROUP CONNECTION ☐
SLEEP ☐
FUN ☐
_____ ☐
_____ ☐
_____ ☐

MEDITATION DOWNLOADS

NOTES / THOUGHTS / MUSINGS

 WHAT INSPIRES YOU?

INSPIRED DOODLES

DRAWINGS /SKETCHES /DOODLES

WHAT INSPIRES YOU?

F *
YEAH,
YOU DID
IT!!

A++
GOLD
STAR
YOU
DID
IT!

JUST IN CASE...
HERE ARE A FEW EXTRA PAGES

Be a Proud Member of the "Reset Club" Resetting can be a great experience... no worries, it's all good!

DAY

ALCHEMY **100** Challenge

GRATEFUL 4'S:

TODAY I WANT TO:

....

be	feel	think
....	....	....
....	....	....
....	....	....

ALCHEMY MEDITATION NOTES:

DIGITAL DETOX AM ☐

MEDITATION AM ☐

30 MINS MOVEMENT ☐

FOOD ☐

WATER ☐

OUTDOOR MOVEMENT ☐

DIGITAL DETOX PM ☐

READ 10 PAGES ☐

GROUP CONNECTION ☐

SLEEP ☐

FUN ☐

_____ ☐

_____ ☐

_____ ☐

ALCHEMY 100 Challenge

DAY

ALCHEMY 100 Challenge

GRATEFUL 4'S:

TODAY I WANT TO:

....

be

feel

think

....

....

....

....

....

....

....

....

....

ALCHEMY MEDITATION NOTES:

DIGITAL DETOX AM ☐
MEDITATION AM ☐
30 MINS MOVEMENT ☐
FOOD ☐
WATER ☐
OUTDOOR MOVEMENT ☐
DIGITAL DETOX PM ☐
READ 10 PAGES ☐
GROUP CONNECTION ☐
SLEEP ☐
FUN ☐
_____ ☐
_____ ☐
_____ ☐

ALCHEMY 100 Challenge

DAY

ALCHEMY 100 Challenge

GRATEFUL 4'S:

TODAY I WANT TO: ....

be	feel	think
....	....	....
....	....	....
....	....	....

ALCHEMY MEDITATION NOTES:

DIGITAL DETOX AM ☐
MEDITATION AM ☐
30 MINS MOVEMENT ☐
FOOD ☐
WATER ☐
OUTDOOR MOVEMENT ☐
DIGITAL DETOX PM ☐
READ 10 PAGES ☐
GROUP CONNECTION ☐
SLEEP ☐
FUN ☐
_____ ☐
_____ ☐
_____ ☐

DAY

ALCHEMY **100** *Challenge*

GRATEFUL 4'S:

TODAY I WANT TO:

....

be	feel	think
....	....	....
....	....	....
....	....	....

ALCHEMY MEDITATION NOTES:

DIGITAL DETOX AM ☐
MEDITATION AM ☐
30 MINS MOVEMENT ☐
FOOD ☐
WATER ☐
OUTDOOR MOVEMENT ☐
DIGITAL DETOX PM ☐
READ 10 PAGES ☐
GROUP CONNECTION ☐
SLEEP ☐
FUN ☐
_____ ☐
_____ ☐
_____ ☐

DAY

ALCHEMY **100** Challenge

GRATEFUL 4'S:

TODAY I WANT TO:

....

be	feel	think
....	....	....
....	....	....
....	....	....

ALCHEMY MEDITATION NOTES:

DIGITAL DETOX AM ☐
MEDITATION AM ☐
30 MINS MOVEMENT ☐
FOOD ☐
WATER ☐
OUTDOOR MOVEMENT ☐
DIGITAL DETOX PM ☐
READ 10 PAGES ☐
GROUP CONNECTION ☐
SLEEP ☐
FUN ☐
_____ ☐
_____ ☐
_____ ☐

DAY

ALCHEMY **100** Challenge

GRATEFUL 4'S:

TODAY I WANT TO: ....

be	feel	think

ALCHEMY MEDITATION NOTES:

DIGITAL DETOX AM ☐

MEDITATION AM ☐

30 MINS MOVEMENT ☐

FOOD ☐

WATER ☐

OUTDOOR MOVEMENT ☐

DIGITAL DETOX PM ☐

READ 10 PAGES ☐

GROUP CONNECTION ☐

SLEEP ☐

FUN ☐

_____ ☐

_____ ☐

_____ ☐

ALCHEMY 100 Challenge

DAY

ALCHEMY **100** Challenge

GRATEFUL 4'S:

TODAY I WANT TO:

....

be   **feel**   **think**

....

....

....

ALCHEMY MEDITATION NOTES:

DIGITAL DETOX AM ☐
MEDITATION AM ☐
30 MINS MOVEMENT ☐
FOOD ☐
WATER ☐
OUTDOOR MOVEMENT ☐
DIGITAL DETOX PM ☐
READ 10 PAGES ☐
GROUP CONNECTION ☐
SLEEP ☐
FUN ☐
_____ ☐
_____ ☐
_____ ☐

MEDITATION DOWNLOADS

NOTES / THOUGHTS / MUSINGS

WHAT INSPIRES YOU?

INSPIRED DOODLES

DRAWINGS /SKETCHES /DOODLES

WHAT INSPIRES YOU?

Made in the USA
Middletown, DE
01 October 2023

39542429R00144